PRESENTED TO

....

BY

....

ON THIS DATE

....

QUIET WHISPERS FROM *God's Heart*

FOR WOMEN

CHERI FULLER

COUNTRYMAN

FOREWORD

*I*n the pages ahead you'll read how God whispers to ordinary women. Sometimes He whispers through His Word and other times through singing birds, autumn trees, or a blue heron on the beach. He can speak through a friend, through a book, through a crying infant, or through His still, small voice in our minds.

God whispers to women of all ages and in all seasons of life: high school and college girls, mothers and grandmothers, working women, single women and married women. As I talked to the women in these stories I discovered that while God spoke to some in their quiet times of devotion, more often He whispered in the middle of their life experiences.

One thing is sure—when God whispers from His heart to ours, something changes. Healing begins or an attitude is transformed. A relationship is restored. We're infused with hope and energy when we're just about out of steam. Sometimes God whispers vital direction for a job or other change in life. And sometimes His whispers are meant simply to reassure us of His love.

My prayer is that the stories, quotes, and Scriptures in this book will encourage you to listen and know that God wants to speak to you. He is speaking all the time, but sometimes the clattering culture around us drowns Him out.

Pay attention when He taps you on the shoulder in the middle of your drive time or while you're at your computer or taking a walk. God doesn't waste words. He can change your life with but a few. As you listen and respond to His quiet whispers, your heart and life will be blessed beyond imagination.

CHERI FULLER

Acknowledgments

I want to gratefully thank all the women who were kind enough to share their stories of how God whispered to their hearts.

Many thanks to my editor, Terri Gibbs, for her skill and creativity, to my publisher, Jack Countryman, and my agent, Greg Johnson, for the opportunity to work on this project, and most of all, to God our Heavenly Father, who delights to speak to us, His children!

It is in lonely solitude that God delivers His best thoughts,
and the mind needs to be still and quiet to receive them.

CHARLES R. SWINDOLL

*A*nne packed her bags and tucked her Bible and letters in the worn suitcase. As a young woman, she had left Scotland in the 1930s to serve as a missionary with the China Inland Mission. Now, after nine years, she was going home. In only a few days she would be back with her family and friends. A steamer waited in the Shanghai harbor to take her and the other missionaries home for a long-awaited furlough. As she closed her suitcase and picked it up to leave, Anne heard a clamor outside the mission compound and peered out the window.

Japanese soldiers were goose-stepping in unison down the street, knees almost up to their noses. The thud of their steps echoed in the street, accented by the clatter of their rifles and equipment. It was the first sign of war, and

Anne felt a rush of panic.

But just then God spoke to her heart. *"Listen to Me Anne. You're not going home. You're going to be a prisoner of those soldiers."*

"How long will this last, Lord?" she asked. "Will I ever see my family again?"

He simply answered, *"I will be with you, Anne. Ask me what you will."*

A deep sense of God's nearness and peace filled the frightened young woman. Although Anne had never given her teeth a second thought, she felt urged to pray that her teeth

I do not ask to fly above the storm and sing. Just let me in the tempest feel the covert of Your wings!

ALICE
MORTENSON

would be preserved, that not one of them would fall out. So out of obedience rather than vanity, she asked God to protect her teeth.

Moments later soldiers were at the door herding men, women, and children out into the street. Anne and the other missionaries were marched hundreds of miles to a Japanese prison camp.

There she spent three and a half years enduring near-starvation, bitter cold in winter, and scorching heat in summer. Cruelty, rats, disease, and death were all around her. But God's quiet whispers encouraged her heart and helped her keep a sense of humor, even in the worst situations.

Forty years later Anne shared her stories with me over lunch. Her eyes twinkled as she remembered the joy of God's constant presence and provision for her in that prison. After World War II ended, Anne was released. Although she was in extremely poor health, every single tooth was preserved.

God had remained faithful, constantly merciful and loving even in the midst of terrible circumstances. Although Anne's losses weren't over (her mother had died during the war and many uncertainties awaited her), God's whispers of encouragement and hope carried her well into old age as a woman not of bitterness, but of peace and wisdom.

"We went to Turtle Creek yesterday and the azaleas, tulips, daffodils were glorious!" my sister raved. As I hung up the phone, my mind flashed to the lush pink and red azalea bushes I'd seen every spring growing up in Dallas. My kitchen windows were blank and dark. Even if I could see through the Maine evening, I would only find barren trees, grungy snow, and frozen ruts in a muddy road.

The next morning I walked down the lane near our house. Everything was frozen. The bare trees stood stark against the white fields. The sky was gray . . . again. In the entire month there had been only twenty-four hours of sunshine—something very depressing for a transplanted Southern girl. My soul felt as drained and gray as the sky.

Just then I noticed a rose bush that had been severely cut back. Ice was frozen solid around its branches. That forlorn rose bush reminded me of our family. *We've been pruned, too.* I thought. *We're 2,000 miles away from family and friends. Holmes' building projects are on a downhill slide.*

Our savings are gone, and money is tight. We hadn't found a church to be involved in . . . we feel disconnected and useless.

In the midst of my thoughts God seemed to whisper. *"Like the rose bush, you will bloom again and be fruitful if you sink your roots deep into Me. This rosebush wasn't cut back by accident. Someone pruned it purposefully so there would be abundant roses next summer. Trust Me in the winters too!"*

God did bring us through that long winter, and as we saw Him provide again and again, when we were down to "pennies on the dining room table" as our kids called it, our trust in Him deepened. We grew a hardy endurance and perseverance as Holmes worked an all-night job at a printing press and I substituted at the high school by day and wrote magazine articles at night. God taught us invaluable lessons, like thanking Him for the gift of life itself and for our children's smiles as they played in the woods behind our house.

By the next spring, though we still faced many difficulties, we were back home in Oklahoma. Eventually, Holmes had construction projects again, and God opened new doors for me in writing and speaking. Slowly, imperceptibly at first, the blooms began to appear. As surely as God had promised, spring did come again.

> *Though the fig tree may not blossom, Nor fruit be on the vines; Though the labor of the olive may fail, And the fields yield no food . . . Yet I will rejoice in the LORD!*
>
> **HABAKKUK 3:17-18**

aroline has an unusual job for a young woman. She manages a night shelter for the homeless in Bedford, England. A shelter she sometimes describes as "my house of lovely criminals!"

Naive at times, Caroline can still be shocked when she finds out exactly who has been staying with her.

One day, a police officer telephoned and inquired whether George was staying at the shelter. "Yes," Caroline answered, "George has been here for some time."

"Then you'd better be extra cautious. He is a known sex offender."

The next time Caroline saw George, she struggled to love him as freely as she had before the telephone call. Instead of love, compassion, and forgiveness, she discovered fear, anger, and judgment lodging in her heart.

A short while later, Helen came to the shelter. Caroline's heart softened during a long conversation with the homeless woman. Caroline liked her immediately and looked forward to ministering to her. Then shortly after Helen left the shelter, Caroline was stunned to read in the newspaper that her latest resident had just been arrested for serial murder! Caroline felt so vulnerable. *I've entertained a murderer! How will I feel when I see her again? Will I be able to feel compassion for her?*

The memory of Helen and George stayed with Caroline. Talking to a friend a few days later, she shared what a struggle it was to love people when she knew the horrible things they had done. "It's so hard to look at them and love them. Instead, I look at them and judge them."

In the middle of her sentence, she heard God's passionate whisper, *"Caroline, I see all your offenses, and I still love you—unconditionally!"*

From that moment Caroline began praying that God would empower her to love others—even murderers and rapists—without condition. Just as God loves her!

But God demonstrates His own love toward us,
in that while we were still sinners, Christ died for us."

ROMANS 5:8

Love, expressed in kindness,
permits us to unfold.
BECKY FREEMAN

or all of us, there are times in our marriage when the joy disappears and so much distance grows between us and our mate, we wonder if we will ever be happy again. Becky and her husband, Scott, had hit such a roadblock in their marriage. They'd visited a marriage counselor, read all the right books, and tried to implement the suggestions, but nothing helped. They were both fighting for their rights and had their own ideas about how their problems should be solved. Instead of growing closer, they were growing more distant and lonely.

But one afternoon their relationship completely turned around—all because of a simple ham sandwich. They were on vacation and Becky was lying in the beach engrossed in a novel. All of a sudden, someone was standing over her blocking the sun. It was Scott, with that sweet smile she still loved, offering her a ham sandwich. Just white bread and deli ham, but somehow it spoke volumes to her heart . . . not just about food, but about Scott's love for her.

She swallowed the lump in her throat, and thanked him for the sandwich. They sat there on the beach, sharing a Dr. Pepper and a simple picnic lunch. Later they went back to the hotel room, poured out their sorrows and misunderstandings, and fell into each other's arms. The walls crumbled between them and their delight in each other took a giant leap forward. Once again, Becky felt secure in her husband's love and care and was able to understand his needs more fully.

Who would have thought God would whisper healing love through a simple ham sandwich?

inda's baby daughter lay in a coma in an ICU hospital bed, following a car accident. Instead of sleeping in the guest bedroom of her parents' home, Linda kept vigil in ICU, perched on a stool, clutching her baby's hand.

The nuns who ran the hospital were compassionate and offered to let Linda sleep in one of the empty rooms on a floor the hospital was remodeling.

Linda gladly accepted. Every night, around midnight, she rode the elevator down to the deserted floor, walked down the dimly lit hall and into her room before twisting the flimsy lock and pushing several pieces of heavy furniture against the door.

Even if someone tries to break in, these security measures will give me time to telephone for help, Linda reasoned.

One night Linda rode the elevator down to her floor but found the room locked. She walked back to the empty nurse's station in front of the elevator and called security. "We'll be up to unlock your door in just a few minutes," the security guard assured her.

She sat in the abandoned nurses' station, waiting for the guard. As she waited, a still, quiet voice spoke to her spirit.

"Get up, walk across the floor, and stand by the wall," it seemed to say.

She shook her head sleepily, not wanting to budge from the comfort of the padded chair. *What a silly idea. From that vantage point, I won't be able to see inside the elevator when the guard arrives.*

Again she heard the voice, this time more insistent. *"Get up, walk across the floor, and stand by the wall."*

Slowly she left the desk and began to walk to the wall. Passing the elevator, she saw the red glow of the down arrow. The doors began to slide open.

At last, she thought, *the man from security has finally come to let me into my room.* She continued walking toward the wall. Her tennis shoes didn't make a sound. Suddenly the elevator doors slid open. Looking back, she tried to see who was inside, but was too far down the hall. *Well, where's the guard? I can hear him breathing. Why doesn't he come out?*

When Linda reached the wall, she stopped and turned around. The elevator doors were now wide open and a yellow light spilled onto the floor of the darkened foyer. She started to walk back the way she had come, when the elevator doors suddenly slid shut.

Before she could catch a glimpse of the guard, the elevator shut with a clang. Bewildered, Linda stared at her dim reflection in the closed doors. *Why did I act so strange? If I had stayed at the nurse's station, I could have greeted the guard when the elevator doors opened. He would be opening the door to my room right now.*

She called security again and was assured that someone would be there shortly. Linda rested her head on the desk. A short while later she was startled by the scurry of footsteps and blinked sleepily as two nurses rounded the corner. They stared in surprise.

"What are you doing here?" a male nurse asked gruffly.

"I'm waiting for a security guard to let me into my room."

"You'd better come with us!" the female nurse responded. "There is a stalker in the hospital tonight. He's attacked several women. It's not safe for you to be alone."

The color drained from Linda's face. Suddenly it all made sense. The man in the elevator had NOT been the security guard. She had almost come face to face with a potential rapist. If she hadn't obeyed God's quiet whispers, she might have been attacked.

How glad she was that she had listened to that divine whisper. And how glad she was to know that God's divine presence was with her even in the midst of tragedy as she continued to wait ten long months for her daughter to awaken from a coma.

ne sun-kissed morning, Laura wandered down the tree-covered sidewalk in her neighborhood. Burdened by the demands on her day, she talked to God. "Lord, why doesn't my life have more joy? You promised us 'joy unspeakable,' but I can barely manage an occasional smile."

God spoke to her in a quiet whisper. Very clearly the word *expectations* popped into her mind.

"Expectations? I don't understand, Lord. What do you mean?"

Suddenly clear thoughts filled her mind. *"Remember when you were a little girl? You were always dreaming about what your life would be like when you grew up. You would*

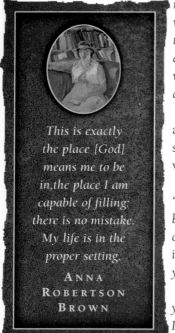

marry a man like your dad; you would have two handsome boys and two darling girls; you would live in a cottage with red geraniums at the window; you would spend your days canning peaches from your orchard."

"But Lord, what are you getting at?" Laura interrupted. "I'm not sure what my lack of joy has to do with expectations."

His answer was perfectly clear. *"When you went to college you left behind your childhood, but not your childhood dreams. Hanging onto imaginary expectations has stolen your joy . . .*

"You expected a husband like your dad, who could fix anything. But I chose a pastor to be your husband;

> This is exactly the place [God] means me to be in, the place I am capable of filling: there is no mistake. My life is in the proper setting.
>
> ANNA
> ROBERTSON
> BROWN

one who would fix his
eyes on me and preach
and teach my Word.
Unlike your dad who
can mend broken
fences, your husband
was called to mend
broken hearts . . .

"You expected two
little girls to dress up
with ribbons and bows.
But I entrusted you
with five boys. Instead
of putting bows in little
girls' hair, I've called
you to put my Word in
the hearts of young
men who will grow up
to be mighty warriors for my kingdom . . .

"You expected a cottage in the country, but I gave you a
four-bedroom home in the suburbs. Your cul-de-sac is filled
with children who need to know my love."

Laura paused at the edge of the forest, stunned by
God's words. Yes, she had to admit it. "I have stolen my
own joy. I wanted You to give me an easy life instead of a
profitable life. Forgive me, Lord. And help me to trust You
and the plan You have for my life. Your designs are far
superior to my dreams."

As she turned toward home a glow suddenly filled her
heart. Perhaps the joy had been there all along—hidden
under that heavy load of *expectations*.

*M*om organized and planned everything—meals for two weeks, our weddings, her garden. She never went to bed unless every dish, piece of cloth, and towel was washed, dried, and put away. She wrote our names on the underside of the furniture designated for each of us and divided her jewelry among us five girls "so we wouldn't squabble." Two weeks before she died of cancer, she asked me to write down the songs and Scriptures she wanted for her funeral— her "graduation" or "glorious homecoming," as she called it.

"I want 'Great is Thy Faithfulness,' Evie's 'Special Delivery,' Psalm 121, and Revelation 21," she told me. I wrote everything down. "Oh, yes, and don't forget that little chorus you sing." Mom was referring to "Beauty for Ashes," a chorus from Isaiah 61 that speaks of God giving us beauty for ashes, the oil of joy for mourning, the garment of praise for the spirit of heaviness. Whenever Mom was feeling low because of another radiation treatment, that was the song she asked me to sing. It seemed to lift her heart.

"Be sure that song is sung at my service," Mama said again, "and if no one in the choir can sing it, promise me

> *God helping you:*
> *Take your everyday,*
> *ordinary life—*
> *your sleeping,*
> *eating, going-to-*
> *work, and walking-*
> *around life—*
> *and place it before*
> *God as an offering.*
>
> **ROMANS 12:1**
> *The Message*

you and the kids will sing it." You don't argue with your mother when you're taking final directions for her funeral service, so of course I agreed.

Two weeks later, after Mom died, I gave her instructions to the pastor. The next day he called and said, "Everything's planned just as your mother wanted it, but there's one problem. No one in the choir has ever heard of that song "Beauty for Ashes.'"

I sang a few stanzas, showing him how the song went. "Surely someone in your choir can sing that simple melody."

"Unfortunately, nobody feels comfortable singing it on such short notice. If you still want it to be part of the service, I guess you'll have to do it."

The day of the funeral I woke heavy-hearted and exhausted from all the weary nights at the hospital. In my quiet time I prayed, "God, I can't do this. I'm not a professional singer and I'm definitely not in any shape to sing at Mama's funeral . . . but I don't want to break my promise to her."

I turned the pages of my Bible and began to read Romans 12:1: "…present your bodies a living and holy sacrifice, acceptable to God, which is your spiritual service of worship" (NAS). God seemed to whisper, *Just make yourself available to me, and I'll do the rest.*

Later that day at Mama's service, banked by sprays of red roses and white carnations, my husband and I and our three kids stood up and sang the little chorus from Isaiah 61. Our voices rang out clear and true. Yes, God did "do the rest." He gave me the strength to sing the promised song—and a willing family to sing along with me.

One morning while Connie was getting ready for work, her attention was captured by the sound of birds singing in the trees. It wasn't unusual in the spring, but this time it seemed that God was tapping her on the shoulder, directing her to stop and really listen.

She was struck by the thought that God wants so much for us to find and enjoy music that He has filled the air with it. He also wants us to create music for ourselves, to be creators of beauty—like He is.

An appropriate Scripture in Genesis came to mind. "And Adah gave birth to Jubal . . . he was the father of all those who play the lyre and pipe." *Did God smile when Jubal created his own small flute?* Connie wondered.

Going downstairs, she opened her journal and wrote:

> **Then**—*You said, "Let us make music and fill the air with song." So you poured the stuff of sunshine and morning stars into small throats. And it was good.*

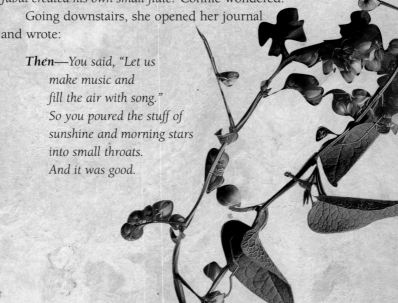

Now—*It's spring and I'm putting on my shoes.*
Listen. The air is thick with flying echoes
of creation song.
A wonder moment with God.
Notes for the taking.
Song snatches to birth creation in us.
And it is good.

As Connie listened to the concert of bird songs throughout the day, it seemed that God was speaking to her heart. *"The bird song is My doing. I put it there for your enjoyment and pleasure."*

Such a small thing, an everyday blessing, but as she pondered the music of the birds it gave her a new appreciation for the gift of music, for the generous mind and heart of God. What incredible care He took to fill the place we live with beauty and with song.

The little blond fourth-grader stood at the door of a run-down house with bullet holes in the siding.

Jennie was waiting eagerly to be picked up for Whiz Kids, a tutoring program for at-risk, inner-city students. Her mom was in a psychiatric ward for drug addiction and depression. Jennie needed help with reading, and I was assigned as her tutor.

That night was the first of many throughout the school year that we spent together. We read aloud, wrote stories, played educational games, and practiced vocabulary words. Then after listening to Bible stories with the other Whiz kids, I drove her home. It didn't take long for us to become fast friends.

After Jennie graduated from the Whiz Kids program I missed seeing her. But I was busy with writing deadlines, speaking engagements, and family and church responsibilities. Over the next few weeks I continued to pray for Jennie, but God interrupted my prayer time one morning to suggest that perhaps that was not enough. *"The program has stopped, but your work with Jennie hasn't. She needs someone to encourage her and help her on a long-term basis."*

Suddenly exciting ideas flooded my mind. *Why not sign her up at the public library for the summer reading program and take her regularly so she continues to build her reading skills? I can have her over to the house to make muffins and share our Sunday lunch. I'll give her books and encourage her to turn off the television and read. I'll take her on walks and invite her to church.*

This year, Jennie is in the sixth grade. Her home situation hasn't changed, but she has moved out of the at-risk category in school. She loves to read and is active in Sunday school, memorizing Scripture and enjoying Christian friends. We still go on long walks and enjoy doing crafts together. Jennie's dreams of going to college and having a home in a safe neighborhood become more possible with every step she takes in the right direction. God has a marvelous plan for her life, and I'm so glad He encouraged me to put feet to my prayers so I could be even a small part of it.

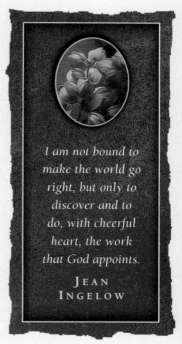

I am not bound to make the world go right, but only to discover and to do, with cheerful heart, the work that God appoints.

JEAN
INGELOW

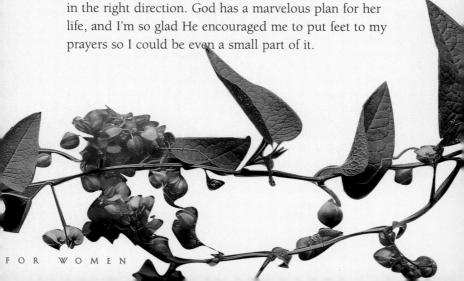

*G*eorgia dashed upstairs to her room at the conference center and grabbed some notes for the seminar she was presenting. It was only the first day of the conference, but already she felt caught up in the whirlwind of activities, workshops, and time pressures. On her way out the door, she glanced quickly out the window across Chesapeake Bay and noticed a blue heron standing on the shore. Elegant and beautiful, the heron's long neck jutted out as it moved slowly along the shore. The bird paused gracefully between each step, like a bride walking down the aisle.

It was the end of October and there were no people on the shore—just an incredible stillness, water shimmering like diamonds, and the stately blue heron. Looking out at the sea and the bird, Georgia heard God whisper, *"You were going so fast you almost missed the beauty of the heron. Stop and watch—notice how it doesn't strive or hurry."* It was a Father's gentle admonition. *"Be still, and know that I am God"* (Ps. 46:10).

As she watched, mesmerized by the scene, Georgia felt the tension melt away. Her spirit settled as she realized what a direct contrast the heron's deliberate movement was to the fast-paced whirlwind of the conference—and to much of her life. Caught up in busyness, she was missing the beauty around her.

In a matter of moments, God had adjusted her priorities, almost like a spiritual chiropractic alignment. For the rest of the conference and for weeks afterward, the image of the lovely blue heron came to her mind, reminding her to slow down and be still, to brush off the clamoring hurry of the world.

Let thy soul walk slowly in thee,
As a saint in heaven unshod,
For to be alone with silence,
Is to be alone with God.

SAMUEL MILLER HAGEMAN

eloved Christian author and speaker, Catherine Marshall learned one of her greatest lessons of obedience from insomnia. Because she suffered from chronic sleeplessness, her doctor prescribed sleeping pills. After years of taking the pills, Catherine felt God questioning her dependence on them. But she ignored His persistent warnings, afraid He would ask her to do something she didn't want to do. Besides, she desperately needed sleep to get her writing done the next day!

One day when she was boarding an airplane, she realized she'd left her bottle of sleeping pills at home. Thinking this was how God was going to give her a breakthrough with her insomnia, she asked Him to let her sleep naturally. But that night, sleep wouldn't come. She tossed and turned all night—and came face to face with just how dependent she was on the pills.

On the way home she inquired, "Lord, am I hearing You right on this? Do you want me to stop using these foolish little pills?"

"*Yes,*" God whispered to her heart. "*The pills are foolish. But the real issue is—you want sleep more than Me. Lay your desire for sleep on the altar, Catherine. Give it to Me. I have great blessings in store for you.*"

Taking a courageous step and hoping for a miracle, Catherine threw all her sleeping pills away and informed God she was going to depend completely on Him for

Emotional peace and calm come after doing God's will and not before.

ERWIN W. LUTZER

sleep. But for eight days and nights, she couldn't sleep. When she did, she had terrifying dreams about rejection and danger. During the day she was exhausted and nervous; at night she was miserably awake.

"Lord, I obeyed you, and look what's happened! I'm worse off than before!" she wailed.

Again God gently assured her, "*You want the instant miracle of sleep on demand. I'm interested in healing the whole person.*"

Finally, on the eighth night, Catherine was able to sleep. Not only did she sleep soundly, she dreamed of God's steadfast love and care. He brought healing not only to her insomnia but to the deep fears of rejection and danger she'd suffered all her life. Catherine's road to freedom, both from sleeping pills and inner turmoil, led through the door of obedience to God's quiet whisper.

here's no such thing as a mistake in drawing," Melissa's elementary art teacher told the class. "So don't try to erase all your blunders. Every squiggly line, every misplaced circle, or splotch of color can be made into something creative and new." Then with a few skillful strokes of her paintbrush, she showed the kids how to change what looked like a messed-up painting into a work of art.

Since then, there have been lots of botched and squiggled canvases in Melissa's life: mistakes and messes of her own making or hurtful things she's experienced because of the mistakes of others. Sometimes she's tempted to sink into regret and think, *If only I could erase that . . . if only it hadn't happened, my life would be so much better.*

But in those times, she hears God whisper that although He doesn't erase history, He can use even our mistakes and the mistakes of others to create something beautiful—if we bring all the squiggled lines and broken pieces of our lives to Him, admit our mistakes, and ask for His help.

Can God change something ugly or broken into something beautiful? There's no sin, grief, or heartache so great He can't bring something good out of it, if we'll let Him. We may see only the sorrow or crisis in our lives . . . we may feel only the ache of defeat . . . but He can bring beauty even out of a heap of ashes (Isaiah 61:2).

If an earthly artist can save a botched drawing and turn it into something lovely, how much more can God's love and power redeem every mistake in our lives. Hurts and losses become bridges for us to reach out and comfort others. Dreams that died are brought to new life. Weaknesses become blessings because they draw us closer to Him.

Can God create beauty out of mistakes? He specializes in that kind of art!

> *We know that all things work together for good to those who love God, to those who are the called according to His purpose.*
>
> ROMANS 8:28

odi's husband, Bill, left for Vietnam in October. Flying helicopters only fifty feet above the jungles, he faced danger from enemy ground fire daily. Married just a year and a half, Jodi was now living with her parents. She missed her husband immensely and with a major Viet Cong Tet offensive coming up in January, she grew more fearful every day. While Bill was in battle in Southeast Asia, Jodi was battling her own enemy— *fear*—and was losing.

Paralyzed by anxiety, she didn't want to stay at home because she was afraid a telegram informing her of Bill's death might arrive. If she left, she might return home to the worst news of her life.

Jodi kept all her fears locked up inside; not even her parents knew how fearful she was. She asked God for peace in her heart and for Bill's safety, but the truth was she didn't feel she deserved Bill and saw no reason why she should be spared grief when so many other wives were losing their husbands. When a younger cousin stationed in Viet Nam died, she attended his funeral and spent time with his grieving family, which caused her fear to escalate. And every night the newsreels on

> *The Holy Scriptures tell us what we could never learn any other way: they tell us what we are, who we are, how we got here, why we are here and what we are required to do while we remain here!*
>
> A. W. TOZER

television announced more deaths. Would Bill be the next one?

One night as Jodi was reading the Bible, she came upon 1 John 4:18, "We need have no fear of someone who loves us perfectly; his perfect love for us eliminates all dread of what he might do to us" (TLB).

That's me, she thought. *I'm dreading what might happen to me and worrying whether God will take Bill.* It was as though God put His finger on the page and said, *"That's what you're afraid of."*

The passage continued: "If we are afraid, it is for fear of what he might do to us and shows that we are not fully convinced that he really loves us." In that moment God whispered, *"You don't believe I love you. You don't believe that even if I take Bill, I still love you and have a plan for your life."*

Suddenly Jodi realized that the problem was more than her fear of Bill's death and the dangers he faced in Vietnam. It was a lack of trust in God and His love for her. As the truth of His Word sank in, she knew she could trust Him—with her husband, with her life, with everything. From that moment on, the issue was settled. Peace replaced fear.

Although Bill didn't come home for many months, Jodi was no longer afraid of tragic telegrams or telephone calls. She quit worrying and started trusting.

This experience transformed Jodi's spiritual life. She learned that God could minister to her by His Word and His Spirit. Never again would she forget that He cared deeply for her and would meet her every need—she simply had to trust Him.

walked around the block that had been our neighborhood for the last three years. We had bought our first house there, had wallpapered the kitchen and breakfast room a cheerful yellow print, grown red roses in the garden, and built a wonderful fort for the boys in the backyard. It was home to our two sons and our brand new baby. I had started a playgroup with other moms who became my close friends, and for the first time in our marriage I felt truly at home.

Sadness filled my heart at the thought of our impending move. I wanted to be like Abraham who said "yes" to God's call to travel to unknown places and live as a stranger camping in tents because he was keeping his eye on an unseen city with eternal foundations —the home designed and built by God Himself (Heb. 11:8-10). Although I sensed that God wanted me to be flexible instead of being stuck on some earthly dwelling, I was struggling.

Lord, You know I'm a nester by heart. I'd just love to stay right where we are. I don't even need to move the furniture to be content, much less change houses.

If you find yourself loving any pleasure better than your prayers, any book better than the Bible, any house better than the house of God, any table better than the Lord's Table, any person better than Christ, any indulgence better than the hope of heaven— take alarm!

THOMAS GUTHRIE

As I mentally wrestled with God about why we were making this move, He gently whispered, *"Yes, I know you'll miss the house, but remember I am your dwelling place— not the house you live in or the rooms where you eat and sleep. You'll live in other houses here on earth, but don't get attached to any of them; they are all temporary. I am your permanent dwelling place!"*

Fortunately, I had no idea how many other houses God was referring to! When we moved again last summer for the ninth time, storing some furniture and giving our children other pieces, I heard God's gentle reminder once more, *"I am your dwelling place."* It makes me grateful, too, for the home He's making me in heaven— where I'll never have to pack again!

tephany was a brand-new Christian. Young and single, she enjoyed a great career working with commercial photographers. But the Monday morning after she gave her life to Christ, she walked into the studio and felt an overwhelming sense of "darkness." She had always known the photographers were involved in a wild lifestyle, but it hadn't kept her from working with them. Now, all of a sudden, she heard God's voice. *"You need to get out of here. I'll provide something better for you."*

Stephany didn't even know God talked to people. But His message was unmistakable. She left the job immediately, with no other prospects for work, and eventually found a position in sales for a fitness club. As the months went on, she desperately missed photography, but the only job she found was in a department store portrait studio. She toyed with the idea of accepting the position. It wasn't her first choice, but at least she would be behind a camera.

However, in her prayer time, God spoke to her again. *"I want you to go to Mr. Graves* (the vice-president of the fitness club) *and ask him for money to start your own photography business."* She thought, *"I must be thinking bizarre thoughts. I barely know Mr. Graves. How could I ask him for money?"*

Reluctant to approach him, Stephany tucked the message away in her heart and kept working. One morning soon after, the vice-president called and asked her out to breakfast. He had heard she was quitting and wanted to know why. Stephany explained that what she really wanted to do was photography. In the next breath, he offered to loan her enough money to get her business started and suggested she come by his office the next day—there might be some equipment she could use. In the closet she found a 4 X 5 view camera, lights, and power packs (things most people don't just have sitting around!). With the equipment and the loan, she was ready to set up her business. She agreed to work for the health club another six months, so the loan was quickly paid off.

The wind of God is always blowing . . . but you must hoist your sail.

FRANCOIS FENELON

A short time later, as she was walking down the street, a gentleman she had worked with through another photographer stopped her. "I'm working for the newspaper now. Maybe I could get you an article."

From that Sunday paper news feature, Stephany's photography business took off. But God didn't leave her to her own devices. When she worked on lighting set-ups and had no idea how to do it, she'd say, "God, please help me find an answer; show me the way to do this," and He walked her through it, step by step. As her business grew, it was clear that God had done just what He said—provided something better, much better than she could ever have asked or dreamed.

*C*aylon's husband, Bob, lay in the hospital for a week because of internal bleeding. After the bleeding was stopped, the doctor came in and gave them the diagnosis: ulcerative colitis. "Colitis of this sort is often triggered by stress," he said. "I don't know what stressors you have in your life, but you need to eliminate them as much as possible."

With her husband in a weakened condition, Caylon thought she had an audience and began to lecture him about what she thought should be done. "The cows, chickens, pig, and other animals—we don't eat them. They're just pets that have to be taken care of. They take too much of your time. They've got to go!" She was sure the animals were the source of Bob's stress.

"This is a good time for you to get rid of all those animals," she continued. "They do nothing but sap your energy when you've already put in a full day of work."

Too weak to argue, Bob responded, "Okay, whatever."

Caylon was sure he would get rid of the animals as soon as he got out of the hospital, and she became increasingly frustrated when he didn't. One day she walked past the bay window with its clear view of the barn and spotted Bob sitting on the ground, surrounded by a menagerie of animals. The cow and chickens were eating out of his hand. God froze the scene before her and whispered, *"Does that look stressful?"*

God's gifts put man's best dreams to shame.

ELIZABETH
BARRETT
BROWNING

Caylon stood riveted at the window. For the first time she saw her husband through God's eyes, saw that this was how Bob enjoyed unwinding after a hard day of work. Bob looked as relaxed as she'd ever seen him. No, the animals weren't the stress in his life . . . perhaps her attitude was. Caylon realized that she had been drawing conclusions based on her perspective rather than God's. But God saw Bob's heart and had provided what satisfied him.

It was a lesson she never forgot. With her heart and eyes open, Caylon began to ask God for His perspective on other matters about her husband and found her marriage slowly transformed. Even the animals became a shared enjoyment.

God speaks to us through His creation. Through nature, through song. He reaches one person one way, and another in other ways. He reached Caylon through some chickens and a cow.

It's amazing how a little thing can cause a big conflict. A little thing such as my teenage daughter's hair! It had become a power struggle between us. She wanted to be creative—to try a shorter style, dyed burgundy. I envisioned a horrid red hue spoiling her long, lovely blond hair, and since I was paying for her beauty-shop expenses, I thought I ought to have a *little* input. Naturally, she disagreed, and tension grew between us over the hair issue.

Strangely, tension also grew between the Lord and me. Frustrated, I prayed, "Lord, what do you want me to do? You know what she'll look like with those colors!"

One day soon after my prayer God whispered distinctly to my heart, *"Release her . . . and her hair."*

Now the struggle was in my spirit. Only God's power could help me to obey that quiet whisper.

Finally, one afternoon when Alison was in the kitchen, I turned to her and said, "Ali, your hair is yours to do with whatever you want. So is your room. And though we'd prefer that you keep it clean, there is going to be no more nagging or picking up after you."

> *Don't exasperate your children by coming down hard on them. Take them by the hand and lead them in the way of the Master.*
>
> **EPHESIANS 6:4**
> *The Message*

With a smile, she agreed. While I wasn't thrilled with her messy room or all the creative hairdos and colors she paraded to the breakfast table each morning, transferring responsibility to Alison provided one less opportunity for conflict.

I was comforted one day when I heard Dr. James Dobson say, "I'm convinced the pulling away of adolescents from their parents is *divinely inspired.*" With relief, I realized Alison's attempts to be more independent were entirely normal. It meant that I needed to let go—and entrust her continually to her heavenly Father.

When I released Alison and let go of control, she began experimenting with her own hair and even colored and cut her friends' hair. Right away she showed tremendous talent, and this year she's attending hair design school. Now she's cutting and highlighting *my* hair . . . and doing a beautiful job, I might add!

After the surprise birth of her daughter, Lynn felt God leading her to leave an exciting twenty-year career. She fretted over this wrenching decision, clinging desperately to comfortable surroundings, a respectable income, professional friends, and lots of recognition. Lynn worried that she would sink into depression in the isolation of her home, deprived of interaction with colleagues and meaningful work.

Patiently, God began to pry loose her grip. One weekend as she walked in the autumn woods, she watched the colorful leaves cling tenaciously to branches, struggling to hold on. Then with each gust of wind, as if by God's command, they simply let go. Beautiful and free, they entered a graceful waltz, pirouetting with abandon in the breeze.

At that moment God whispered, *"Lynn, let go!"*

Later that week she gave her employer notice and committed to enter whatever "dance" God was choreographing for her.

Soon, however, it was wintertime outside—and it felt like winter in Lynn's heart. Depression, doubt, and loneliness ensued as she struggled to adjust to life without her career. Yet again God spoke to her through nature. Like a winter tree, she was stripped of the lush foliage of professional purpose, accolades, and friendships. But though the winter tree looks dead, it is alive; the leaves are gone but life remains in the roots. Likewise, as she rooted herself in God and His Word, her life would be fruitful.

Trees don't fret. They bloom in season, and in times of barrenness raise their leafless limbs in praise to their Maker. Stripped of foliage, they behold the stars shining like brilliant jewels between their branches.

> *[She] shall*
> *be like a tree*
> *Planted by the*
> *rivers of water,*
> *That brings forth*
> *its fruit in*
> *its season.*
>
> **PSALM 1:3**

Lynn took a lesson from the trees. She decided to stop fretting, to look instead for the stars twinkling between the branches of her life. And each day she discovered a host of luminaries, blazing constellations of joy to record in her journal:

Wednesday—Thank you, God, for the joy of Sheridan, my precocious four-year-old imp, who just interrupted my quiet time for the tenth time in fifteen minutes. She is precious, playful, observant, sensitive, and darling—in addition to being as delicate as fine bone china with roses painted in her cheeks. Thank you for this "gift and reward" (Psalm 127:3) and the time to enjoy her.

Friday—Thank you, Lord, for our second ballet class today with Miss Reneigh. It was sheer joy to see Sheridan flit like a tiny, pink butterfly across the floor—I wouldn't have missed it for the world!

*I*n a few days Steve would board a plane for a three-week business trip to Taiwan.

"Honey, why don't you and the children fly over and meet me in the Philippines?" he asked Susan. "I can show you where we lived, my old boarding school, the church mom and dad planted . . . it'll be a great family time."

I don't know the language. I'm afraid the kids will get sick. What would I do with two active preschoolers on a sixteen-hour plane ride? Besides, it's too late to get passports and tickets, Susan thought. Steve had been a missionary kid in the Philippines, whereas Susan grew up in Los Angeles and had never traveled farther than Disneyland. She knew it would be important to Steve to show her the country where he spent his childhood, but in her mind they simply couldn't do it. *We could be exposed to terrible diseases; we could get kidnapped or get parasites. It's a nice idea . . . but we simply can't do it.*

Susan was convinced the issue was settled, until she ran into her pastor the next day. He inquired about Steve's upcoming trip and asked if she was going along.

"Well, Steve wants us to go over in two weeks, but it's impossible," she told him.

"I really think you should consider going," the pastor answered. "Think what it would mean for Steve to share the foundations of his life with you." Through his words, she felt God nudging her out of her comfort zone. She thought about their missionary friends in the Philippines. Maybe they would like a visit.

Later that day she thought about her cousin, a travel agent. With one call, the cousin obtained tickets, and called her lawyer-husband, who got the ball rolling for passports. Even the hurdle of having to get official birth certificates for the children was handled in one day, and instead of getting the passports in weeks, they came the day before the family was scheduled to leave.

God had truly parted the sea for Susan. The kids slept the entire fifteen hour flight, and the missionary friends met her at the airport in the Philippines. A few days later Steve arrived.

Back in the country where he grew up, memories flooded his mind. He told Susan and the children story after story from his childhood. They visited the river where he fished, the field where he played ball, the boarding school where he studied, and the church his parents built.

No one got sick. The kids were terrific travelers. It turned out to be the best trip their family had ever taken . . . but almost missed . . . until God whispered through a friend.

> *Every act of trust makes the next act less difficult, until at length, if these acts are persisted in, trusting becomes, like breathing. . . .*
>
> HANNAH WHITALL SMITH

Our son was in the pediatric wing of the hospital fighting for his life. Only moments before, the doctor had called us out into the hall after examining our six-year-old and said, "We've done everything we know to do for Justin. Something inside his body has got to rally." He had suffered a severe asthma attack the day before. Though the doctors had always managed to get his breathing under control with high-powered medications, on the day he was to start first grade, his life was in jeopardy.

Stunned, I couldn't believe what I heard. My heart raced and fear overwhelmed me. My husband sent me home to reassure our other two young children and to try to "pull myself together" since I was a nervous wreck and only making things worse. Dashing through the driving rain in the parking lot, I tried to find our car. Finally, soaked and shivering, I gave up and went back into the hospital to wait for the storm to let up.

Finding refuge in the chapel, I was drawn to a large white Bible by the altar. There I read the words, "Why are you downcast, O my soul? Why so disturbed within me? Put your hope in God, for I will yet praise him, my Savior and my God" (Psalm 42:11, NIV).

Downcast . . . disturbed. That was me. In the quiet I prayed, *Lord, I've put my hope in the wrong things. That's why I'm so afraid; I've trusted you in some areas of my life, but I've clung to my kids, trying to keep them safe. I feel like your disciples out in the boat that stormy night who cried "Master, we're*

Lord, still my anxious heart to calm delight— for the Great Shepherd watches with me over my flock by night.

RUTH BELL
GRAHAM

*perishing!" Lord,
I feel like I'm
perishing too!*

Quietly an
inner voice
whispered to
my heart. *"Cheri,
where is your faith?
Trust in me . . . be
still."* Just then,
lightning caused
the chapel lights
to flicker off and
on, and thunder
boomed outside.
The raging storm
reminded me
that God was
the Creator
of the whole

universe. If He could command a thunderstorm, surely He
could handle my son's life.

I bowed my head and gave Justin back to God. As I
sat in the silent chapel a huge weight began to lift off my
heart. The icy fear that had gripped me melted away. I
knew that Justin was safe and cared for, that I could trust
God . . . whatever happened.

Justin did defeat that battle with asthma, and though
he faced many others in the years to come, after that
moment in the hospital chapel, his illness never again left
me panicked and despairing. Like the storm, my heart was
at rest. God was in control.

arcia had never felt so alone in her life. It didn't matter that her two young daughters giggled as they raced noisily through the house. It didn't matter that she was making good money in real estate.

What mattered was that her husband had left her—alone. Alone with no family nearby to help. Alone with the burden of parenting. Alone in a house she could no longer afford. Alone with the guilt and grief of a failed marriage.

Numb from the stress of a twelve-hour workday and the responsibility of caring for her girls at night, Marcia didn't have the strength to go on. The intense pressure piled up until she felt herself breaking into a million little pieces. Desperate for help, she called a local hospital. "I feel like I'm having a nervous breakdown," she said. "Could I come there if I can't make it through the night?"

When you come to the point where He's all you have, you realize He's all you need.
ANONYMOUS

She could.

Comforted by the assurance of help, Marcia postponed going to the hospital.

She went instead to the Great Physician. Opening her Bible to Isaiah 61:2-3, Marcia read that Christ had come to heal brokenhearted people like her, that He could turn her mourning into joy and exchange the heaviness she felt for a thankful attitude.

As she read those words, God whispered, *"I've been with you all along, Marcia, even when you weren't aware of My presence. When there's no one else, I'm right here with you. I am your Helper."* The words were like healing salve poured over her aching heart, and for the first time she realized the enormous strength that was available to her in Christ. She knew with confidence that God would be with her in all the challenges she faced.

Through His guidance, she left a position in commercial real estate, which took her away from her daughters until after dark every night, and started a house–cleaning business. Not only did she make more income, but she was able to be home for the girls after school.

The five-bedroom house they lived in had to be sold and it was badly in need of repair. Since houses in the area generally stayed on the market for one to two years and sold for $10,000 less than the asking price, Marcia's house needed to be in top condition. Amazingly, the same woman who lacked strength to get through the day just a few weeks earlier, with the help of one girlfriend, took off two layers of shingles, installed a new roof, laid a new kitchen floor, and painted the house inside and out. With those improvements, the house sold for a good price, and she was able to buy a nice home she could afford.

Looking back, Marcia realized that had she wasted her energy on worry and emotional distress, she would never have accomplished so much. God's words of hope late one night made all the difference.

ollowing her release from a German concentration camp at the end of World War II, Corrie ten Boom began traveling around the world to share a message of God's love and faithfulness in spite of the horrors of the war. Corrie's busy schedule of speaking engagements and meetings was exhausting. Many times she felt overwhelmed with ministry obligations. There was so much to be done, and she was elderly. She wasn't as strong as she'd been years before. She felt weighed down with *responsibility.*

Feeling especially burdened one afternoon, she poured out her heart to God, sharing her frustrations, worries, and concerns. Quietly, through the middle of her desperate pleas, He whispered, *"Corrie, have you surrendered completely to Me?"*

"Of course," she answered, "I have surrendered myself 100 percent to You."

"Then you don't possess anything anymore, Corrie." He reminded her. *"You are only a steward of what I give you. You aren't responsible for all of this, I am. Obey Me and follow Me, and I will be your victory, your strength, your all."*

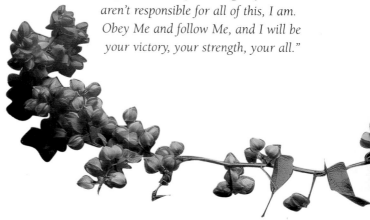

Corrie understood what God meant. His words carried her thoughts back to the concentration camp, where she had owned nothing but the clothes on her back—where she had no responsibility, where she was totally dependent on His care. That had not been her choice, of course; it wasn't a voluntary surrender. But God was reminding

> God sees not only what He is doing, but what will come of what He is doing.
>
> **CHARLES SPURGEON**

her now of a different surrender, a happy, blessed surrender of her life and all she had into His loving hands.

She didn't have to feel overwhelmed and burdened by responsibility. God's ability, wisdom, and love, working through her, would accomplish the work. His assurance filled her with incredible rest and peace. She smiled to herself, *What a relief to depend on God's power and ability instead of my own!*

*I*n high school, Melanie's deepest desire was to be a writer. She desperately wanted to go to college and major in journalism or creative writing, but nobody in her family had ever gone to college and, financially, it seemed a far-fetched dream. She heard of a school-work program, however, and thought that might be her ticket to the university. But there was a problem— when she signed up, the only job left was a nursing assistant's position at the local hospital, and Melanie didn't want to have anything to do with a hospital, much less work in one.

Melanie was torn. A traumatic childhood injury that required daily trips to the hospital, month after month, made her dislike anything or anyone associated with medicine. But she didn't see any other way to get the money for college, and she did want to be a writer, so she decided to give it a try.

The first three months at the hospital Melanie came home and sobbed every night. But when she moaned to her mom about how much she hated nursing, her mother encouraged her to stick it out for three months. By that time, Melanie was coping although it was a grueling schedule. She worked as a nurse's aide from 6:30 a.m. to noon, then went to school from 1:00 to 5:00 p.m. In the summers she was assigned to the night shift . . . but anything to become a writer.

By the second semester of her sophomore year, Melanie was hoping and praying for a scholarship, but her grades weren't high enough. The only offer she received was from the doctor's wife she worked for—with one condition: she had to study nursing. Now she really was in a dilemma. There still wasn't enough money for college, even with what she had made in the high school work program. Her only chance at college was to pursue nursing.

A Sunday school teacher had once taught Melanie that if she ever needed wisdom, she should ask God. Since a decision on the scholarship had to be made soon, every afternoon after school, she changed clothes and walked to a cow pasture at the end of her block. Climbing over the fence, she sat under a tree and prayed. "Lord, I don't know what to do. I want to be a writer, but I've been offered a scholarship in nursing. I want to know what You want me to do with my life. I want to hear what You have to say." After an hour of sitting there, she didn't hear a thing from God. So she went back the next day for an hour, and the next and the next—for two weeks.

Finally, one afternoon God whispered the answer to her question. *"I'm calling you into nursing now. In your later years, you'll write."*

So Melanie gratefully accepted the scholarship and went to nursing school. She graduated with honors and worked as a critical–care nurse for sixteen years. Then in 1985 she resigned her position at the hospital and the next month began to study writing under a local author. In less than three years, she won a national writing contest. Before long she was writing magazine articles on a monthly basis, and eventually God added books.

Melanie hears God regularly now. But she knows she would never have heard His plan for her life if she hadn't been willing to sit quietly in a cow pasture and listen. She was seventeen years old when she heard God's quiet whisper for the first time, but at age forty-nine, those words are still directing her life.

*I*t was one of those Christmases when the schools didn't dismiss until late December. Amy was teaching high school and the frenzy of giving finals had left her little time to enjoy the season. She planned to join her husband and three-year-old daughter who had already traveled to her mother-in-law's home, where they would spend the holidays. Amy considered herself a veteran flyer, nevertheless, she was relieved to have one of the back seats, statistically the safest seats on the plane.

Laughter is God's medicine, the most beautiful therapy God ever gave humanity.

ANONYMOUS

Like most of the other passengers, Amy was just dozing off when the captain announced that they would be going through some turbulence. He asked the flight attendant to take her seat. *No problem* Amy thought as she cinched her seat belt a little tighter. There were a couple of grumbles throughout the plane, but people were too tired to really care.

No one was ready for the terrible jolt that caused the plane to dropped suddenly, leaving most of their stomachs at the previous altitude. The plane went way up, then slammed down, then up again. Amy had never experienced turbulence like this. Anxiety was heightened when all the lights went out, and they were sitting in almost pitch black. She looked out at the wing, lit by a clear night's moon, and was sure it was going to snap right off from the pressure. She gripped her seat and closed her eyes, "Please, Lord, don't make my little girl spend this Christmas without her mother. Please let all of us reach our loved ones safely."

In the midst of the terror, from somewhere in the front of the plane, came a giggle. With the next jolt the giggle turned into a little girl's hearty laugh, and with each subsequent dip and rise the laughter grew into one of those uncontrollable belly-laughs that only a child can produce. Row by row the feeling of unabandoned joy seemed to creep throughout the plane. Soon the child's laughter infected all the passengers, and their groans turned into oohs and ahhs like those on a roller coaster ride. People were laughing and sharing smiles with each other and were almost disappointed when the ride smoothed and the captain announced they were clear of the turbulence.

The plane quieted down, and then, without warning, someone in the dark began to sing. "Silent night, holy night . . ." As strangers joined their voices together, peace and hope surrounded them all.

When they landed safely a short while later, Amy was one of the first to get off the plane. She never did catch a glimpse of the little girl with the infectious laugh, but was sure God had sent the child to ease their burdens and replace their fears with peace. A Christmas gift from heaven you might say.

Teach us to pray. Teach us to live. Teach us to escape the worries of this world, to live and rest in You. The private prayers we pray at midnight are the prayers we live in the morning.

HARRIET CROSBY

When I was thirty-six years old and processing the loss I felt when my mother died of cancer, I found that not only did I miss *Mom*, but I missed the nurturing influence of an older woman—someone who was farther along on the journey and could share her wisdom.

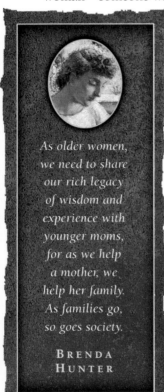

> *As older women, we need to share our rich legacy of wisdom and experience with younger moms, for as we help a mother, we help her family. As families go, so goes society.*
>
> **BRENDA HUNTER**

When one of the kids lost a tooth or became ill, I found myself picking up the telephone to share the news with Mom or to ask for her prayers. As the reality of her passing sank in, God quietly whispered to me. *Look around. There are other mothers, spiritual moms I have provided along your path. Don't miss them!*

I began to notice the older women God had placed in my life. There was Flo, an elderly widow from church. Chatting over a pot of steaming raspberry tea she told me that shortly after meeting us, God had instructed her to bring our family into her circle of prayer and intercede for us daily, as she did for her own children and grandchildren. That was twenty years ago and her prayers continue to this day. When I visited Flo, she wanted to hear all about our three kids (just like Mom) and never got bored with the details of Chris' college plans, Alison's mission trip, or my writing projects.

There was Billie, a shut-in I visited, who always gave me encouragement, prayer, wisdom, and tea. There was Patty, a friend in her sixties who celebrated each day in a colorful and zany way. Once when I was overwhelmed with the task of packing our belongings to move, Patty appeared at my door with boxes, sturdy tape, and white paper. She talked enthusiastically about new beginnings and the positive aspects of changing residences (it's an opportunity to clean out closets and get organized!) and prayed with me about our move. Then she suggested, "Get going on your packing—one box at a time!" Her motherly encouragement made all the difference in my attitude.

When I think how these and other women have touched my life, God seems to whisper to me. *Look around you. What younger woman needs a motherly touch? A word of concern or a prayer from the heart?* God has many mothers, grandmothers, and daughters in the Body of Christ. Perhaps you need one. Perhaps you can *be* one.

No two persons see people and things alike. What we see and how we see depend upon the nature of our light.

LAURA INGALLS WILDER

*A*t a time when she was busy with her flock of little ones, aged three, two, and six months, Connie began to realize that she and her husband, Stan, were not parenting the same way. He had a different temperament and gifts, and a distinctly different parenting style. But Connie was a professional; she had years of experience with children as a Child Life Specialist in hospitals. She'd taken many courses on child development. In fact, she had a Master's Degree in the field. She was sure *her way* was the right way to handle their children. If only her husband would change and do things *her way.*

One day in frustration, she sat down on her bed and began to pray about the conflicts they were having. "God, when are You going to show Stan that *I'm* doing this right, and he should come on board and do it *my way?*" she asked.

As clearly yet quietly as she'd heard anything from God, He whispered, *"If both of you were exactly the same, one of you wouldn't be necessary!"* She knew she didn't want to be the parent who wasn't needed, nor did she want Stan to be expendable.

With those few words from God's heart, a dramatic change took place in Connie's attitude. She began to value her husband's parenting style instead of criticizing it. She began to appreciate his gifts and unique way of relating to their kids, to celebrate their differences instead of being irritated by them. As a result, they had more unity and harmony as parents and a happy peace descended on their home.

or ten years Annette and her husband tried to have children. As the disappointing months and years wore on, she suffered through every kind of infertility treatment and medication, only to have the doctor's offer little hope.

Finally, on her thirtieth birthday, Annette sat in her gynecologist's office and watched as he looked through her thick folder of medical records, then gazed up at her intently and suggested that she accept the fact that she would never have children. Tears flowed down her cheeks.

Through all the years of heartache and disappointment, Annette had always dealt with the problem by herself. She had never turned her need over to the Lord publicly, asking for help from others. But the next day, during a women's meeting at church, she broke down and asked for prayer. "I need to know if I should give up on having children and go on with life. I desperately need God's His peace . . . whatever the outcome. I can't go on like this anymore."

An older woman knelt before Annette and poured out her heart to God. She asked Him to grant the desires of Annette's heart. Like Hannah, she begged God to open Annette's womb and give her a child. As the woman prayed, Annette wept openly and when the prayer was over she felt an overwhelming sense that God had heard the prayer and would answer.

> *For this child I prayed, and the LORD has granted me my petition which I asked of Him. Therefore I also have lent him to the LORD; as long as he lives he shall be lent to the LORD*
>
> 1 SAMUEL 1:27-28

When she returned to work, she told her co-workers about the woman's prayer and how confident she was that God would answer. Knowing her inability to conceive, they poked fun at her.

Yet three days later, Annette and her husband did conceive —not one baby, but twins. As she continued working at the university, she soon discovered that Carol, a college student who worked part-time in the office, was also pregnant. They shared comments about their morning sickness and Annette encouraged the young girl. One morning a few weeks later, God told Annette distinctly to take her favorite book on the development of an unborn child to work with her. "What for, Lord? I've already spent hours pouring over the pictures."

"Just take the book to work," she seemed to hear.

Although Carol had the day off, around lunch time she stuck her head in Annette's office to say hello. When Annette saw her, she knew immediately that the book was meant for her and put it in her hands, "I wanted you to have this book so you could see what your baby looks like."

Carol walked silently to a back office and poured over the book.

The next morning she called Annette and said, "I had an abortion planned for yesterday afternoon, but after seeing your book, I couldn't go through with it. I've decided to have the baby."

Months later, there was cause for great rejoicing not for one or even two—but for *three* little ones, born into the world on the wings of a prayer and a whisper from God.

Although attractive and happily married, Kathy struggled with deep feelings of rejection. She was desperate to be included in whatever social function was going on—luncheon, party, or someone's birthday. If she heard about a gathering she hadn't been invited to, she felt as though an arrow was piercing her heart. Hurtful words would dominate her thinking. *"You're not accepted. You don't have enough money. You're not spiritual enough or smart enough to be included with other Christian women."*

One day as she was driving along, mulling over a dinner party she had just heard about—and had not been invited to—she prayed, "God, it's not like people pick me out and say I'm not good enough or intentionally reject me. I know it's just that they're not choosing me, but it still hurts."

At that moment God whispered to her heart and said, *"But I chose you."*

God chose me . . . God chose me . . . She pondered that thought all the way home. They were simple words, but they began to heal the wounded places in her heart. When she got home, she looked for Bible passages on being chosen, and with each one, the reality that God had chosen her brought a new sense of security to her

> *Jesus, My Lord, is a wall around me. Dwelling within, I can dwell secure; Nothing can harm me, for naught can reach me Save what He willeth that I endure.*
>
> **ANNIE JOHNSON FLINT**

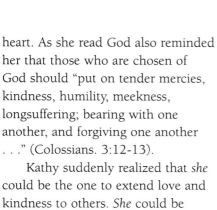

heart. As she read God also reminded her that those who are chosen of God should "put on tender mercies, kindness, humility, meekness, longsuffering; bearing with one another, and forgiving one another . . ." (Colossians. 3:12-13).

Kathy suddenly realized that *she* could be the one to extend love and kindness to others. *She* could be the one to forgive and offer peace. From then on, whenever she heard about events she wasn't included in, her response was different. "That's okay. I didn't need to be there anyway. I'm okay with that." Instead of thoughts of rejection or self-condemnation she thought positive, uplifting things. No longer was her heart wounded, for God's simple words had given her hope and happiness.

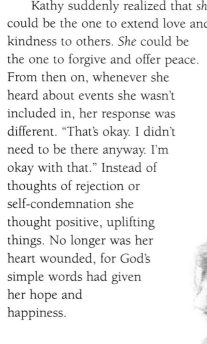

*H*ave you ever responded "Later!" to a child's discovery of a spotted, green crawly creature? Or a giant white cloud that looks just like a dragon? Perhaps on your way to adulthood your sense of wonder and awe faded and was replaced by busyness and practicality, or work and worries.

Mine did. With the addition of each of our children, my schedule got more hectic. I supervised school activities, homework, and sports. I juggled writing deadlines, volunteered at church, and helped in my husband's business. But I was missing the small miracles God placed along my path. I wanted to share in my children's joy and sense of discovery . . . but there was so much to do!

Finally, quite frustrated, I asked God, "What can I do?"

Quietly He seemed to whisper, *"Go fly a kite!"*

"Oh, Lord," I replied, "that seems so silly and impractical."

"That's the point!" He responded.

So I went to the toy store and bought a kite to fly at our next family outing in the park. Chris and Justin enjoyed the challenge of getting the kite up to catch the breeze, and Alison loved having her turn to fly it, but eventually they all got bored and ran off to play. I was left holding the string.

As the bright red and blue kite swept up and flew almost out of sight, my spirits soared. The breeze blew my hair, and a fresh sense of wonder blew over my heart. I forgot all the things I needed to accomplish and reveled in the blue sky, the huge cascade of clouds. Then, as I gazed up, there it was! A spectacular double rainbow! A double promise, a double blessing.

Flying the kite not only refreshed my spirit but pointed me upward, toward God, who knew what would make my heart sing.

*My heart leaps up
when I behold
A rainbow
in the sky.
So was it when
I was a child,
So be it when
I am a man,
Or let me die.*

WILLIAM
WORDSWORTH

ne evening at a speaker's training seminar, Lael and the other participants were invited to share prayer requests. When Lael's turn came, she asked for wisdom for her writing and speaking ministry. Ann, the leader, spoke up from across the room, "I'd like to pray for you, Lael, that because of your rheumatoid arthritis and difficulties in getting around, God would raise up someone to travel with you and assist you."

That's nice and I appreciate her thoughtfulness, Lael thought, *but that seems way ahead of where I am. I certainly can't afford someone to travel with me.*

The next day, before flying back home to Houston, Lael checked in her rental car and the attendant asked, "How are you going to get to your gate? Why don't you leave your bags in the car and I'll just drive you up to the gate?"

Arriving at the gate, Lael was fumbling with her bulky coat, carry-on bag, and briefcase when the skycap offered, "Why don't you let me put all that in a box for you? You don't need to travel with all that gear!" and relieved her of most of her load. With only her briefcase, Lael looked at her next hurdle—the stairs to the Cleveland commuter plane. How was she going to manage the stairs? Before she had time to wonder any longer, a skycap appeared and whisked her in a wheelchair all the way through the airport, down "pilots only" corridors and a backstairs elevator out to the tarmac where she boarded the plane.

In Cleveland, Lael checked in at the desk and waited for her flight to Houston. Suddenly, one of the gate clerks interrupted her reading and said, "Mrs. Arrington, can we see your ticket?" and walked with it back to the desk. Lael was worried, hoping everything was in order for her flight. A few moments later, the clerk returned, handed Lael a new ticket and said, "We bumped you up to First Class. We thought you'd be more comfortable there."

Relaxing in a roomy First Class seat, Lael could hardly believe her good fortune. In wonderment and joy she watched the brilliant sunshine light up the patchy clouds across the sky. She could almost hear God saying *"Isn't this fun? I'm smiling on you and enjoying watching over you today!"*

Immediately she thought of Anne's prayer request. It certainly did seem that Someone was going before her and preparing people to do things she would never have asked them to do. Lael giggled, realizing that God—or one of His angels—had been her flight partner all the way home!

A few days later, one of her friends called and said, "Don't you have a February event coming up and some speaking engagements in the spring? You know, I have a lot of frequent-flyer miles I'd like to use—maybe I could go with you to smooth your way. Tell me as soon as you're ready to make your flight plans!"

Lael smiled as she thought to herself. *I guess God wants to have some more fun! I could get used to this!*

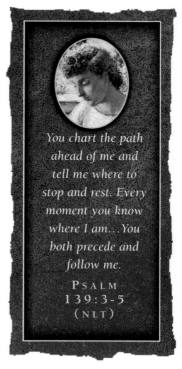

You chart the path
ahead of me and
tell me where to
stop and rest. Every
moment you know
where I am....You
both precede and
follow me.

PSALM
139:3-5
(NLT)

*Before us is
a future all
unknown, a
path untrod;
Beside us a friend
well loved and
known—
That friend
is God.*

ANONYMOUS

missionary wife and mother of four young children, Paula and her family were on their way to the airport with her mom and dad. Their furlough was over. The recurring sadness of leaving parents, siblings, friends, and homeland to serve for four more years in Thailand was overwhelming. And the sight of her four backpack-laden children, a small mountain of carry-on luggage, and nineteen suitcases was almost more than Paula could handle.

Quickly and efficiently her dad pulled the car up to the curb and gave the family orders on what to do. Within seconds they were all outside the airport entrance hugging, crying, and saying good-bye. Then she watched her parents' car speed off down the departure lane. As it disappeared out of sight, Paula stood on the curb feeling totally alone, like an alien . . . with no home in the US and still far from their mission station in Thailand. Her parents were gone, her husband had run into the airport for check-in, and she was left with the sole responsibility of four active, excited kids. Paula's eyes swung around for one more head count, every nerve in her body strung taught with emotion.

Just then, it was as though Someone stood next to her and quietly whispered, *"Fear not, for I am with you; be not dismayed, for I am your God. I will strengthen you, yes, I will help you, I will uphold you with My righteous right hand"* (Isaiah 41:10).

Those words of assurance were just what Paula needed. Suddenly she knew without a doubt that God, who had called her to this unique lifestyle, was with her and would give her strength for the journey ahead.

Two days later they arrived safely in Bangkok, weary but smiling—a dad, a mom, four kids, and all nineteen pieces of luggage!

*V*alerie's son Brian was born with a heart defect. One day when he was only four months old, she was on the way to an appointment with the cardiologist when the baby began crying, stiffened up, and went into respiratory arrest in her arms.

Valerie cried out to God for him to breathe. She prayed with as much faith as she could muster, slapping the baby's back and trying to get him to wake up, all the time pleading with God for Brian to start breathing. She fully expected her baby to take a big breath and be all right, but it didn't happen that way. His little body went limp, he began turning a bluish grey, and Valerie knew he was dying. Her mother-in-law, driving the car, cried out to her in the back seat, *"Do something!"*

As the seconds and minutes ticked by, Valerie began to hear the words in her mind telling her how to help her baby. Although she hadn't been trained in CPR, God gently instructed her how to give Brian mouth-to-mouth resuscitation. The day before, she had watched an exercise show on television that included a segment on how to administer CPR. At the time she hadn't paid much attention, but all of a sudden the words of instruction and pictures from the television screen flashed through her mind, showing her exactly what to do.

When the train goes through a tunnel and the world gets dark, do you jump out? Of course not. You sit still and trust the engineer to get you through.

CORRIE TEN BOOM

Valerie covered her baby's mouth and nose, blew air into his lungs, and waited as his little tummy rose. She watched his tummy fall and gently blew again. A calmness washed over her as she repeated the process. After the fourth breath, Brian's blue eyes opened and he started to whimper, a faint sound like a tiny kitten. The young mother continued CPR until they got to the hospital, where the emergency room team continued life-saving procedures.

The center of God's will is our only safety.

BETSIE
TEN BOOM

Valerie's baby had a long stay in the hospital, but it didn't matter. On that Easter weekend, she and her husband felt God had given their baby new life. The doctor told her, "You did exactly the right thing to save your son's life. I couldn't have done it better myself." Though extremely grateful, she had a nagging frustration with God for not answering her prayer and just causing Brian to breathe on his own that day.

Then one night when she was praying about it, God showed her clearly that He *did* answer her prayer, just not in the way she thought He should. From then on, she knew God was always listening and answering her prayers —but in unexpected, surprising ways, not necessarily in *her* ways.

ometimes God whispers to us during the noise of everyday life, through familiar voices. Jennifer had such an experience one spring day when she and her eight-year-old son were playing a marble game. Because of diminishing eyesight due to a chronic disease, she had to cut the game short.

"Clayton, Mama needs to play a different game. I just can't see to do this anymore." As her son put up the game it was obvious he was in deep thought.

Finally he said, "Mom, I don't think God will heal you here on earth."

Immediately, Jennifer heard the quiet voice of her Heavenly Father say, *"Listen, . . . listen to My heart."* She reflected on what Clayton had said and asked him, "Why don't you think God will heal me on earth?"

He answered, "Because I think God wants you to love heaven more, and if He healed you on earth, you might like earth more—and heaven is best!"

Jennifer knew that God's voice had swept truth through her spirit in the words of her child. Truth she would never forget. Truth that would encourage her in weariness and sustain her through heartache.

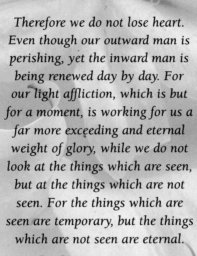

Therefore we do not lose heart.
Even though our outward man is
perishing, yet the inward man is
being renewed day by day. For
our light affliction, which is but
for a moment, is working for us a
far more exceeding and eternal
weight of glory, while we do not
look at the things which are seen,
but at the things which are not
seen. For the things which are
seen are temporary, but the things
which are not seen are eternal.

2 CORINTHIANS
4:16-18

ecause of a severe stutter, Hannah Hurnard was a withdrawn and fearful girl who dreaded people. But when she surrendered her heart to Christ at age twenty, He began to transform her life. She joined the Evangelistic Band and traveled around the countryside holding open-air meetings in the villages of England. She felt that some day she would be a missionary, but she had no idea where she would go.

After four years with the Evangelistic Band, Hannah spent some time in Ireland. One afternoon, she was invited to go with a few friends on an outing to Ireland's Eye, a beautiful spot near Dublin. When Hannah found herself alone on a lovely high peak, she sat on a grassy knoll and took out her Bible. As she read the ninth

chapter of Daniel, God whispered to her, *"Hannah, would you be willing to identify yourself with the Jewish people in the same way Daniel identified with the Israelites?"*

Hannah was upset by the question, for she didn't have any particular liking for the Jews. In fact, she had no desire to be with them at all. "How could I be a missionary to people I don't even like?" she asked.

"If you are willing to go, I will help you love the Jews and identify with them. It all depends on your will," God replied.

Every acceptance of God's will becomes an altar of sacrifice.

HANNAH HURNARD

Hannah knelt on the hillside and told God she would obey. But when she came down from the hills and told her friends about her decision, they didn't share her joy. They thought the idea of going to Israel was extremely unwise. Her doctor also advised that her physical and emotional health would never withstand working abroad, and after writing to the only mission she knew of in Palestine, she was rejected.

But Hannah persevered and eventually did go to Israel. In the beginning, she had to pay her own expenses to travel and minister to the Jewish people, but because of her obedience that day at Ireland's Eye, God launched Hannah Hurnard into a lifelong ministry of evangelism, speaking, and writing that touched millions of people around the world for Christ.

ut of the stillness on a cloudy Monday morning Fran heard the telephone ring. It was her parent's neighbor. "Fran, your mother needs you right away." Fran and her husband quickly rearranged their schedules and drove to the family home. Fear gripped her as they drove.

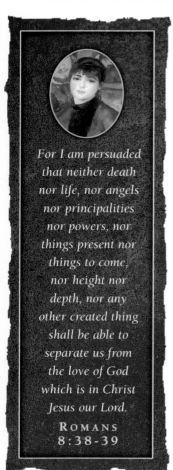

For I am persuaded that neither death nor life, nor angels nor principalities nor powers, nor things present nor things to come, nor height nor depth, nor any other created thing shall be able to separate us from the love of God which is in Christ Jesus our Lord.

ROMANS 8:38-39

Fran had visited her parents recently and was concerned about her dad, a retired mechanic and World War II veteran. Suffering from deep depression, he had been seeing their family physician—the same doctor who had successfully treated him a few years earlier for a similar episode of depression. The family assumed he would recover this time also.

But upon arriving at the house, Fran heard her mother's heart-wrenching sobs. Her dad had shot himself. Fran, her mom, and siblings all struggled with guilt. Believers in Christ, they all loved their dad dearly as the strong, loving patriarch of the family. Now he was gone.

As a nurse, Fran was particularly devastated. Inner accusations consumed her. *If only we'd taken him to the hospital. If only I hadn't*

*been in denial about the seriousness
of his condition. If only . . . if only!*

As Fran walked the long, dark
tunnel of grief, quiet whispers of
God's love helped her to endure.
Through a plaque at a friend's
home that stated "I refuse to
accept responsibility for that
which I cannot control" God
seemed to remind her that she
couldn't direct her dad's behavior.
And during her quiet time one
day, God whispered that she was
responsible for her sins, not for
the sins of anyone else.

God spoke to her again
through a dear friend whose only

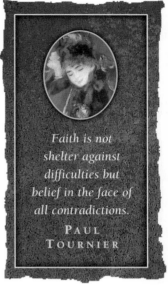

*Faith is not
shelter against
difficulties but
belief in the face of
all contradictions.*

PAUL
TOURNIER

son had died of AIDS. This mother felt like a failure also,
but her counselor reminded her that she alone could never
have caused her son's homosexual lifestyle and subsequent
death—she simply was not that powerful. Fran thought,
"That's true for me, too." Complex factors entered into her
dad's circumstances, and only God knew them all.

After working her way through months of helplessness
and guilt, God whispered again, this time while she was
reading Romans 8:38-39. Through these verses, He
reminded Fran that her dad was no longer depressed but
joyful and at peace. At home! He had left earth much
sooner than they'd hoped, but he was waiting for them
there—in heaven.

atherine drew and painted as a child and went on to study art in college. She grew up in a church, but never committed her life to a personal relationship with Christ. At age twenty-five, however, she was diagnosed with pancreatic cancer. With a three-year-old son and three-months to live, she began to ask some hard questions: *What happens after I die? Is there a heaven? How can I be sure I will go to heaven?*

"God," she prayed one day on the hill by their country house, "are You really there? I don't know if You're real or if You're too big to care about what's happening to me, but I'm really scared. I need You to make yourself real to me."

In the quiet of the night, under a starlit sky, Katherine surrendered her life to Christ. She was drawn to the Bible for the answers to her questions, and the more she read, the more it dawned on her that God truly cared for her and loved her. She realized that if she died, she'd be with Him; and whether she lived or died He would always be with her. She still had a

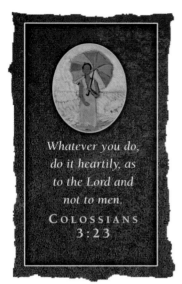

Whatever you do,
do it heartily, as
to the Lord and
not to men.

COLOSSIANS
3:23

major health problem and a troubled marriage to handle, but she wasn't dealing with them alone.

Several months later when Katherine was at the grocery store, she called home and her husband informed her, "Your test results are back . . . they're clear! You're okay!"

In that moment of amazing joy and relief, Katherine heard God whisper, *"I'm giving your life back; now use it to glorify Me."*

Overcome with gratefulness, she wanted to respond, but how could her life glorify God? She had no college education, no money, and now a broken marriage. The only thing she had to offer was her meager art talent. After college she had never attempted to create anything because she was always sure she would fail. But now she gave her talent to God.

Soon after, Katherine created a pastel of a deer. After completing the work, she sold it to a catalog company. It went into publication and sold nationwide, eventually selling more than three million copies.

God multiplied and used her talent not only to provide an income for herself but to bring joy to others as well. She went on to create hundreds of works of art that touched many, many lives. Her "meager" talent, when given to God, did indeed bring Him glory.

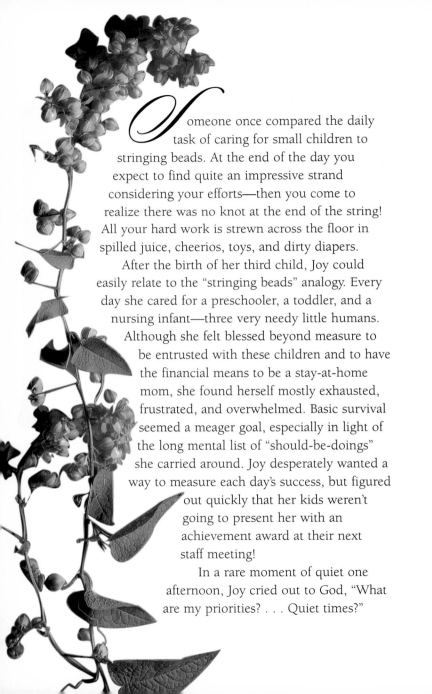

*S*omeone once compared the daily task of caring for small children to stringing beads. At the end of the day you expect to find quite an impressive strand considering your efforts—then you come to realize there was no knot at the end of the string! All your hard work is strewn across the floor in spilled juice, cheerios, toys, and dirty diapers.

After the birth of her third child, Joy could easily relate to the "stringing beads" analogy. Every day she cared for a preschooler, a toddler, and a nursing infant—three very needy little humans. Although she felt blessed beyond measure to be entrusted with these children and to have the financial means to be a stay-at-home mom, she found herself mostly exhausted, frustrated, and overwhelmed. Basic survival seemed a meager goal, especially in light of the long mental list of "should-be-doings" she carried around. Joy desperately wanted a way to measure each day's success, but figured out quickly that her kids weren't going to present her with an achievement award at their next staff meeting!

In a rare moment of quiet one afternoon, Joy cried out to God, "What are my priorities? . . . Quiet times?"

(Those were hard to come by). "Scripture memorization?" (She could hardly remember where she put her purse!) "Exercise?" (How about pull-ups; she would pull the covers up over her head each morning). When she finally took a moment to listen, God led her to Psalm 138:7-8, "Though I walk in the midst of trouble, You will revive me; . . . the Lord will perfect that which concerns me."

"Joy," He seemed to say, *"if you'll quit looking for significance in your circumstances and accomplishments and simply rest in your assignment, I will accomplish My agenda through you each day. This important season of your life may not look like you think it should, but by serving these little ones you are serving Me."*

Sure enough, when she let God's plans dictate her "doings," her life was filled with peace and contentment. Some days that divine agenda consisted simply of three meals and snacks, spills and clean-ups, diapers and laundry . . . but always, God's love.

> *Let your home be your parish, your little brood your congregation, your living room a sanctuary, and your knee a sacred altar.*
>
> BILLY GRAHAM

Six months after Steve's accident, he came out of a coma, began to speak, and was able to recognize people. He laughed at jokes and cried when they sang together. Cindy thought they were on a roll and was hopeful her mate would soon be able to resume a normal life.

But in mid-July his progress slowed again; he had a blood clot in his lungs, underwent surgery for the tendons in his feet, and had increasing trouble communicating. The nurses suggested he might have to be moved to a nursing home.

After a trip to see him at the rehabilitation hospital, Cindy was vacuuming and praying through her tears. "God, I don't get this; I don't understand. You made Steve; you know how he works. And You have the power to *do something* about the condition he's in. It's wasteful for this vibrant, creative father and husband to remain in this state, and *you could do something about this.* But I don't understand why you aren't acting . . . now."

Just then her six-year-old son Tate ran into the house yelling, "Mom! Mom! The big boys are playing basketball, and they won't let me play."

"Tate, they're in the middle of a game right now," she explained. "When they finish, I'm sure they'll let you play."

"But I don't want to wait, Mom! It's our basketball and hoop—why don't you do something about it?" Tate stomped his foot in frustration.

"That's true, Tate. But I'm not going out there and force those boys to include you right now. You'll just have to wait until they're finished with their game. Then you can play."

"You mean you aren't going to do something about it *now?*" Tate said. After realizing his mother wasn't going to budge, he ran out, slamming the door in a huff.

As Cindy pondered their conversation, she realized that Tate didn't have a clue why she wouldn't go out there, stop everything, and get him into his brother's game. He knew she had the power to act and was choosing not to. It seemed cruel and unloving. He couldn't understand that it wouldn't be in his best interest for her to intervene.

His words rang in her ears, and she thought of her husband. Did God have a perspective on Steve's situation that she couldn't understand? Did God's apparent inaction have a higher purpose than she knew? Isaiah 55:8 came to mind: "For My thoughts are not your thoughts, nor are your ways My ways. . . . For as the heavens are higher than the earth, so are My ways higher than your ways, and My thoughts than your thoughts."

As Cindy began to ponder the great gulf between her perspective and God's, she felt His presence and heard Him whisper, *"Trust My ways even though this looks senseless and wasteful. I love Steve more than you, and you've got to trust Me even though you don't see the whole picture. You can be impatient or you can trust me."*

It was a watershed moment. Cindy quit trying to figure everything out and released her timetable to a loving God who had her best interests—and her husband's —at heart. While Steve continued to make tremendous gains, it was a slow and painful process. Gradually, he regained his quick wit, abstract thinking, and creativity (skills the doctors said he would probably never recover.) After nearly two years of surgeries and rehabilitation, their family experienced the most joyful homecoming of their lives.

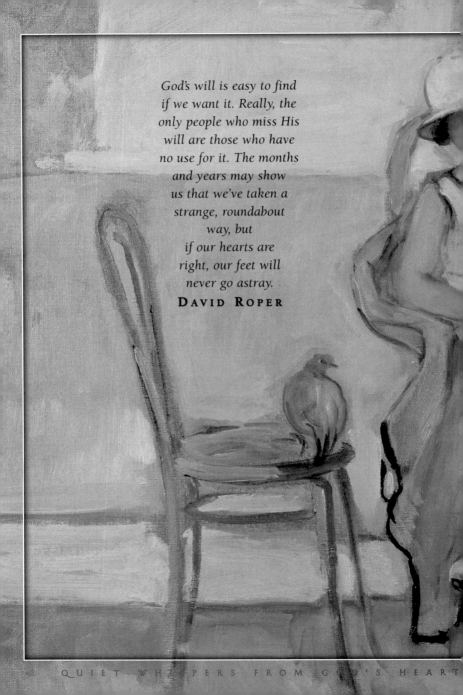

God's will is easy to find
if we want it. Really, the
only people who miss His
will are those who have
no use for it. The months
and years may show
us that we've taken a
strange, roundabout
way, but
if our hearts are
right, our feet will
never go astray.
DAVID ROPER

The six of us kids sat around mom in the long black limousine. Dressed in our Sunday best, we watched as the procession of cars began its slow journey from the red brick church to the cemetery where Papa would be buried. Eleven years old, I felt as if my entire world had fallen apart.

In contrast, other people bustled by in their cars, hurrying to lunch and shopping dates in the September sunshine. Vehicles loaded with businessmen, mothers, and laughing children sped down the highway without a glance at us. Their lives were going on as usual, while ours had changed forever.

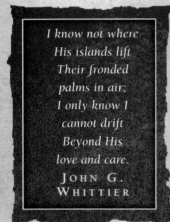

*I know not where
His islands lift
Their fronded
palms in air;
I only know I
cannot drift
Beyond His
love and care.*
JOHN G.
WHITTIER

We drove in silence down a country road toward the cemetery, past fields ready for harvest. A farmer in faded overalls stood between short rows of corn, hoeing with intensity and vigor. When he saw our black limousine, he leaned on his hoe, took off his straw hat, and bowed his head as if in prayer. It was one of the most poignant moments of the entire day for me, a visual reminder that God loved us and cared for us. The respect and compassion the farmer showed in that simple gesture touched my heart and lightened my load of sorrow.

The memory of that man, standing in a Texas field with his head bowed, lingers like the sweet scent of the yellow Tyler roses we placed on Papa's grave. It's a cherished memory of God's love and care—His whisper to my aching heart.

They passed a list around the Sunday school class asking for volunteers to provide food for an upcoming church banquet. By the time Christine got the list, there was only one dish left: a large fruit cobbler. She wasn't excited about doing any of the cooking to begin with, and she certainly didn't want to make cobbler. Out in their little country town, buying frozen cobbler wasn't an option—she would have to make it from scratch.

Christine rebelled at the thought. *I am NOT going to make a big cobbler for all those ungrateful people. They'll just go through the line, pile the food on their plates, and gulp it down. They won't appreciate all the time and effort I'll have to put into making it . . . the homemade crust . . . fresh fruit. Besides, I already spend so much time involved at church . . . more than most of these other women. I'm not going to do this! Someone else can!* But she was the last person available, so there was no escaping.

> God will not ask how many books you have read; how many miracles you have worked; He will ask you if you have done your best, for the love of Him.
>
> MOTHER TERESA

The next week, though still frustrated about being coerced into making the cobbler, Christine went ahead and bought the peaches and other ingredients. The day before the banquet she sliced the peaches and sifted the flour, grumbling to herself all the while over having to do such an insignificant yet time-consuming task. By the time she was making the crust, which kept falling apart and breaking, she was downright angry. With flour dusted

all over her clothes and tears of frustration running down her cheeks, she heard a whisper from God, *"Inasmuch as you've done this unto the least of these, you've done it unto Me."*

Well, no one could deny it, she thought to herself. *This was certainly a "least of these" situation. Folks at the banquet wouldn't know who had taken the time to make their peach cobbler from scratch, and they probably wouldn't care. But if she did it for God, He would know—and He would care.*

Suddenly, making the cobbler didn't seem like an unpleasant duty at all. Her whole attitude changed. No matter how long it took, no matter how crooked the crust, she was glad to be doing it—and a whisper from God had made all the difference.

*S*ending her children off to boarding school was the most difficult thing Lisa had ever experienced as a mother and a missionary in Southeast Asia. Her oldest son, Andy, went for the first time when he was just two months short of his seventh birthday. His first two years away were almost more than her mother's heart

*Speak to Him,
thou, for He hears,
And Spirit with
spirit can meet—
Closer is He than
breathing,
And nearer than
hands and feet.*

ALFRED,
LORD
TENNYSON

could bear. She clung desperately to God's promises for assurance. Two years later, her second son, Timmy, left the "nest," and five years later her only daughter, Amber, left. Although the children attended a wonderful international school, it was still thousands of miles away from home!

Gradually, Lisa learned to trust that God would not only care for them but would bless them. Then just as she was getting the "trust thing" down pat, it was time for Andy to take the next step— go even further away to a junior high school in the Philippines. She felt his despair and uneasiness at being one of the youngest kids in a high school dormitory. The culture was different, and the family living dynamics were foreign to him. His classes were difficult, and he struggled to be accepted in a new social setting.

About that time she was reading the Bible and came across one of God's names in Hebrew, El Roi, the God who sees. In another passage (Genesis 16:11) she read that the angel instructed Hagar to call her son Ishmael, which means "God hears." Like a warm, gentle hug around her troubled heart, Lisa knew God was watching over her son. God knew everything the boy was going through and was there to care for him, because He is Jehovah *Shammah,* the God who is present.

Lisa couldn't be with her son but God was. She couldn't be there to listen to his heartaches, to give him a hug and words of encouragement, but he wasn't alone. God was with him—the God who sees and hears . . . and cares.

Elaine and her husband decided to sell a large house in the city and refurbish a ramshackle, 1920's farm house. Elaine vacillated between the excitement of decorating a new place from scratch to stark panic at the thought of moving into such a small house and all they'd have to do to make it livable. You could see through the floor to the ground; there were layers and layers of old paint and linoleum that would have to come off; and it was going to be a challenge to cover the rotten boards, shiplap walls, and ceilings.

Elaine began the task enthusiastically, armed with stacks of *Country Living* magazines and piles of elegant pictures depicting what she wanted the house to look like. But eleven–hour days in the Texas summer heat soon put a damper on the excitement. Thoughts of the overwhelming task of reconstructing the eighty-year-old house began to fill her mind with panic and fear.

Driving down the bumpy road from her sister's house one afternoon, when construction workers had failed to show up all week and a string of crushing

> *He gives more grace when the burdens grow greater; He sends more strength when the labors increase. . . . When we reach the end of our hoarded resources, Our Father's full giving is only begun.*
>
> ANNIE
> JOHNSON
> FLINT

time pressures had reduced her to tears, she broke down and sobbed, "God, I can't take this any more! We need a carpenter . . . we need an electrician to fix the old wiring so the house won't burn down . . . we need a painter and someone to fix the holes in the roof . . . we need someone to fix the floor . . ."

Elaine gripped the steering wheel, tears pouring down her cheeks, and faced the old house once again. When she stopped the car, through all the panic, turmoil and frustration, she heard God's quiet whisper: *You don't need any of that. You need Me. Don't you think I will take care of you? Just keep doing what you can and let Me do the rest.* She started going over her list of needs again with God when suddenly she realized He didn't want her to focus on her list of requirements and people—He wanted her to focus on *Him.*

God's whisper didn't change one splinter or remove one rotten board in the house, but it did take away the panic and fear. It also helped Elaine to clarify her heart's desire that their "new" home might glorify God. If she was ever tempted to ask "Why God? Why do we have to leave our beautiful house for this tiny one?" she simply looked across the green fields and rolling hills at all the beauty God had provided and her heart was at rest.

When Cathy and Robert moved as college students from New York to Oklahoma, the transition was difficult. But the elderly residents in their apartment complex rushed to their aid, serving them meals, inviting them to ice cream parties, and making them feel part of the family. God used another neighbor to teach Cathy a valuable lesson that changed her life . . . and her spiritual viewpoint.

Sonia, a woman in her late thirties, left an abusive home at seventeen to seek a career in nursing. She wore strange clothes and had long, black greasy hair. At first Cathy and Robert found her difficult to get to know, but over time she slowly warmed up to

> *Give to the world the best that you have, And the best will come back to you.*
>
> **MADELINE BRIDGES**

them. She began knocking on their door to hand them plates of delicious food, saying simply, "I couldn't eat it all myself."

Typical impoverished students, Robert and Cathy didn't have much of anything—not much money or food— yet on days when they planned to open a can of beans until the next paycheck came in, Sonia would suddenly appear at the door with a platter of roast chicken and wild rice. Cathy began to wonder if the woman was an angel!

Once their studies were finished, Cathy and Robert made plans to move to Massachusetts. Shortly before they moved, Sonia and Cathy spent the day together at an arts festival, enjoying the crafts and music and food. Near the end of the day Cathy turned to Sonia and said, "You give and give, and I don't have much to give you. But I'd like to pay you back in some way for all the kindness you've shown us. What do I have that you'd like?"

Sonia smiled at Cathy and answered simply, "You can pay me back by helping your new neighbors in Massachusetts." That was what she wanted in return.

When the couple arrived in Boston and moved into a campus apartment for married students, God often brought Sonia's request to Cathy's mind. When she saw a new single mom, He whispered, *"There's someone you can help"* and nudged her to provide a meal. She found opportunities to do laundry for a sick neighbor and there were always requests for free babysitting from the young couples in the complex.

Then just about the time Cathy began to feel she had paid back Sonia's kindness, God took her a step further. One morning she turned to Romans 12:1 in her Bible. "I beseech you therefore . . . that you present your bodies a living sacrifice, holy, acceptable to God, which is your reasonable service."

Somehow that word *service* caught in her mind. It seemed God was saying that her service to others was a generous sacrifice to Him, an act of worship. Suddenly she realized that every opportunity to serve was another opportunity to worship God. The needs of her neighbors were not intrusions, but potential blessings!

*S*ally's nephew Trey asked her to sing at his wedding —two solos in an enormous sanctuary in front of family and friends, many of whom had never heard her sing. *I sing just fine at our little church in the country, but singing in that big church in downtown Dallas will be another matter!*

"Lord, help me to not get choked up, to get my breath, to sound good . . ." she prayed. She so wanted to shine. But when the time came for her solo, her nerves and the formality of the occasion got the best of her and she lost all voice control. She had a coughing attack and lost her breath right in the middle of the last song. It was a disaster. When it was over she felt humiliated and angry at God. She had asked Him to help her sing, and look what had happened. She wasn't on speaking terms with God for a few days and vowed she'd never sing in public again.

But after a time, Sally was asked to sing for a worship service in their small country church and she accepted. Since she didn't have time to prepare anything new, she sang the same song she had sung for the wedding. That Sunday morning before the service she found herself struggling again with fears when God whispered to her heart, *"Who created you, Sally? Who made your voice?"*

"You made me, Lord," she answered, "and You made my voice."

"Yes, your voice is Mine, and I will use it. It's not for your glory but Mine."

That Sunday morning her singing was totally different. Instead of focusing on herself and her voice, Sally focused on the One who had given her that voice. She felt a new freedom and sang beautifully. The fear that had caused her to lose voice control was gone, replaced by a new joy and confidence—not in herself but in God.

God can do great things with our lives, if we but give them to him in sincerity.

ANNA ROBERTSON BROWN

pulled out of the parking lot at Children's Hospital after spending the morning writing with the children in the cancer center. Cody, his cowboy hat covering his bald head, had dictated to me all the things he was thankful for. Between getting her blood counts and receiving chemotherapy, I'd helped Chandler write a story about her cat, Bruno. And Chris, a sixteen-year-old, had needed some direction for the book he was writing about his battle with cancer.

As I pondered the events of the morning, I heard God whisper, *"This is the time for you to be here. You wanted to be here earlier, but your time doesn't always line up with My time."*

How true! My mind went back six years when I first had the idea to use my experience as a writer to work with cancer patients at Children's Hospital. I thought kids battling cancer might be encouraged by writing a "Someday" book about their hopes and dreams for the future. But alas, when I shared my ideas with the volunteer coordinator and went through the volunteer training, I was appointed to serve coffee in the surgery waiting room. The coordinator said they didn't need me to work with the children; they already had enough people doing that. So I served coffee for a number of months and,

> I said to the man who stood at the gate of the year: "Give me a light that I may tread safely into the Unknown." And he replied: "Go out into the darkness and put your hand into the hand of God. That shall be to you better than light and safer than a known way."
>
> MINNIE LOUISE HASKINS

eventually, because of other demands on my schedule, stopped volunteering.

Recently I had begun to paint ceramics with an old friend, Marcia, and over the weeks she described the art projects she was doing with cancer patients at Children's Hospital. She asked if I'd be willing to help one of the teenagers who wanted to write a book about his experiences, and I agreed. I took my sample "Someday" book along to share the idea with the new volunteer coordinator.

There is an appointed time for everything. And there is a time for every event under heaven.

ECCLESIASTES 3:1(NIV)

Her enthusiastic response took me totally by surprise. "The children would love making these books and writing poems with you! You're just what we need!" I was overjoyed! The ideas were the same ones God had given me six years before, but somehow, in His divine plan, that was not the right time to put them into practice. Now He had swung the doors open wide and had given me a clear invitation to work with the kids.

It caused me to think how we often get frustrated when people aren't open to our ideas or plans, when things don't happen according to our timetables. As I headed home I whispered a prayer, *"Lord, help us to realize there's a right time for everything, and help us to wait for your perfect time."*

*M*any times we see God's hand on our lives quite clearly in hindsight, but there are also times when His presence is so obvious we feel we could reach out and touch Him. Either way, He gently guides, provides, and wraps His love around us.

Jane had never been quite so afraid in her entire life. Her parents had just experienced a financial reversal; they lost their beautiful home and were left with little but the clothes on their backs and a few salvaged possessions. Six months later, she discovered that her husband, a seminary student, was involved in an alternate lifestyle. When Jane realized her husband was no longer committed to their marriage and their few years together had been based upon deception, she was devastated.

[Cast] all your care upon Him, for He cares for you.

1 PETER 5:7

Life became a twisted reality. She'd left a full-time position with a national magazine to move with her husband to another city so he could finish his seminary training, and they'd spent all her savings on his tuition and debts. Soon she found herself with no job and no energy to interview for a new one. Her parents had no means to help, and her husband was leaving her. A believer since age eight, Jane couldn't understand why her life had taken such a horrible plunge.

Yet the darker her surroundings became, the more she was aware that God was with her. Quietly but distinctly, little holes were punched in the darkness and strong streams of light flowed in. With each one God seemed to whisper, *"You're not alone. I'm with you."*

The first stream of light came when she received a telephone call from a college acquaintance who had purchased a historic home and needed help decorating it. When they toured the house, the friend handed Jane $1,500.00 to get her started. Jane didn't even know how she had gotten her phone number. The woman just remembered that Jane had a flair for decorating in college and decided to call. Other streams of light came when an aunt opened her home, a part-time job became available,

and Jane's brother moved halfway across the country to be near her and offer unlimited love and support.

Jane had never felt such tangible and direct answers to prayer. It was as if God Himself had handed her these gifts right from heaven. It was as if He had wrapped His arms around her—which was exactly what He had promised to do.

uth Bell Graham was extremely burdened for her oldest son. Since his teen years he had been running —running from God and from other people's expectations of what he "should" be as Billy Graham's son. He smoked, drank, fought, and was expelled from college. Eventually, he began traveling to distant places around the world, running farther still.

One night Ruth woke up, so alert she couldn't go back to sleep. She lay in bed and, as often happened, became preoccupied with thoughts of her son. *What will happen to him? When will he come home? Where is he tonight?* It wasn't long before she was overcome with worry and apprehension.

Battling her fears and imaginings, Ruth suddenly heard God whisper, *"Stop studying all the problems and start studying My promises."*

She couldn't mistake that voice; she knew it was God. So Ruth switched on the lights, opened her Bible, and immediately saw Philippians 4:6-7: "Be anxious for nothing, but in everything by prayer and supplication, *with thanksgiving,* let your requests be made known to God; and the peace of God, which surpasses all understanding, will guard your hearts and minds through Christ Jesus."

> *If only we would stop lamenting and look up, God is here. Christ is risen. The Spirit has been poured out from on high.*
>
> A. W. TOZER

Don't be anxious about anything . . . pray with thanksgiving . . . As she pondered those words, Ruth suddenly realized what had been missing from all the prayers for her son—*thanksgiving*. Straight away, she set down her Bible and began to worship God, thanking Him not only for her son but even for the heartaches and trials he had brought to her life.

It was as if a light turned on. As her fears completely vanished and her mind rested in God's promises, it dawned on her that worship and worry simply couldn't live together. She could choose to worry, or she could choose to worship. It wasn't a difficult choice to make.

hristmas was rapidly approaching. My daughter, Alison, and I were cuddled on her bed reading the Bible story of the rich man who gained wealth and food and amassed so much hay and grain that he had to build bigger barns for it all. The story said he loved all of his things more than he loved God.

"You see," I explained to Ali, "God can always tell if we love our things more than we love Him. Because if we do, we won't share the things He has given us."

That made sense to Alison, and she reminded me of one of her favorite Christmas traditions— picking out one or two of her favorite toys to give to a child who might not receive a present at Christmas. "I want to give some- one a doll this year, Mom. I guess I could give Shelley (her beautiful German doll) or Newborn (her soft, most precious baby doll) to a girl at the orphanage."

I found the words coming out of my mouth before I could stop to think. "Oh, Alison, not Shelley or Newborn! How about Baby Beth or one of the Cabbage Patch dolls?" (The German doll had taken quite a bit of saving on my part, and Newborn had been part of the family since Alison was a baby. I guess those dolls were my favorites, too.)

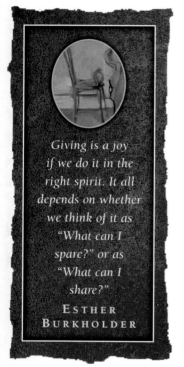

Giving is a joy if we do it in the right spirit. It all depends on whether we think of it as "What can I spare?" or as "What can I share?"

ESTHER BURKHOLDER

"But, Mom, doesn't the Bible say that when we give, we ought to give our best?" Alison asked.

I felt as though God had asked me the question Himself. I was humbled and faced with my own selfishness.

Later that night I prayed: *God, work in my heart so that I will love You far more than all the things of life that seem so important. Help me to find joy like Ali does in giving away my best.*

ynthia had recently been hired by an organization that required its staff to memorize Scripture. A busy college graduate who was beginning a campus ministry and working a second job, she rebelled at the idea of having to memorize Scripture. Still not convinced of the value of memorization, in the third week she finally tackled her first verse, Isaiah 48:17. "Thus says the LORD, your Redeemer, the Holy One of Israel: I am the LORD your God, who teaches you to profit, who leads you by the way you should go."

About the same time, Cynthia decided to apply for a summer mission program in Russia, and the application needed to be postmarked by a certain day. When the deadline arrived, she headed for the post office on her way

to work. With everything necessary for the application —check, application, and envelope —she ran into a shop to copy the application. When she ran back to the car, however, she suddenly realized she'd left the keys in the car! Locked inside were her checkbook and the other things she needed. She had to be at work in a few minutes and wouldn't be out in time to mail her application.

At first she started to panic. But immediately God spoke the recent memory verse to her heart, *"I am the LORD your God, who teaches you to profit, who leads you by the way you should go."* So she said, "Okay, God, I chose to trust that You're directing me. Either You've got a way to get my car unlocked . . . or they'll accept my application even if it's late . . . or maybe I'm not supposed to go."

She walked calmly to her job, leaving her car at the copy shop. A short while later her sister happened to drop by at work— something she had never done— and produced another set of keys for Cynthia's car. Cynthia mailed the application and was accepted for the mission in Russia.

God's might to direct me, God's power to protect me, God's wisdom for learning, God's eye for discerning, God's ear for my hearing, God's Word for my clearing.

ST. PATRICK

Many times, in moments of deadline pressure and frustrating circumstances, God has brought that verse back to Cynthia's mind and reminded her that He is leading her and teaching her—and how valuable it is to hide His Word in her heart.

Once during a time of concern about our ten-year-old son, I found myself becoming overly critical of his attitudes and actions. Chris wanted a pair of black "parachute pants," but we didn't feel he needed them. He was irritated with my reminders to clean his room and stop bugging his sister. I wanted him to talk and he clamed up. I wanted him to change, and he wouldn't. I wanted him to know how much I loved him, and yet irritations pushed us farther and farther apart.

So I began to pray. And the more I prayed for him, the more I heard God whisper, *"You're the one who needs to change. You need to accept Chris just as he is. Don't merely tolerate him but enjoy and appreciate him, ten-year-old quirks and all! There is a time for correction, but this is a time for acceptance."*

Over the days and weeks ahead, I prayed, "Lord, change me! Help me to be a loving and understanding mom. Help me to see Chris through Your eyes."

> *If any of you lacks wisdom, let him ask of God, who gives to all liberally and without reproach, and it will be given to him.*
>
> JAMES 1:5

As God answered that prayer, He worked in both of us. Chris and I started taking time after he got home from school to throw a baseball in the backyard, play a round of ping-pong, or shoot hoops. Even though I usually lost the game and he chuckled at my underhanded basketball throw, my usually quiet son began to open up and share his thoughts with me. He talked about things that

were happening at school: what he was worried about and what frustrated him, what he loved about baseball, what his hopes and dreams were.

As we played and chatted together one day, I remembered the saying "Kids need love the most when they are the most unlovable" and thought that's how God treats us. Long before we loved Him, He loved us. Over the next few weeks God gave us great fun together and brought an acceptance and closeness where there had been criticism and separation. I'm so glad God restored our relationship through a divine "whisper" and didn't let us drift apart.

lison, a registered nurse who volunteered work at a shelter for the homeless in Boston, often spoke to her friend Louise about the work at the shelter. Luoise had a deep concern for the homeless in her town of Portland, Maine. As the two women talked and prayed, Louise felt God guiding her to open a shelter.

So although Louise and her husband, Claude, were both in their mid-seventies, they took their life savings of $50,000 and began searching Portland for a large house. "You'll never find a house for that money. You're too old to start a huge project like this," real estate agents told them repeatedly.

But God said, *"Remember, I've given you this dream, this picture of what I want you to do."* God's voice won out, and find a house they did—a fourteen-room dilapidated structure. Restoring it was a huge project, but as they prayed about how to accomplish it, God directed them to the Cumberland County Jail. After many objections, the city finally agreed to lend them the jail's manpower. With the inmates' help, Claude and Louise restored the ceilings and floors, replaced broken windows, and plastered and painted the entire three-story house.

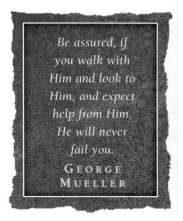

> Be assured, if you walk with Him and look to Him, and expect help from Him, He will never fail you.
>
> **GEORGE MUELLER**

As the completion date drew near they faced many obstacles, but God always provided. Claude, a noted artist, traded one of his paintings for appliances. Their daughter donated a new furnace. Even after the reconstruction, more funds were needed in order to open the shelter. So for weeks, Louise went to churches of all faiths and returned with contributions of blankets, furniture, food, and money.

Finally, the night before Christmas Eve, 1985, Friendship House opened its doors to serve the first of thousands of homeless with a graciousness and love their "guests" (they were never called clients) never dreamed of. God guided Louise and showed her the steps to take, but she did her part to follow His leading.

Sometimes God's whispers launch us into a dream much larger than ourselves. But when we listen for His voice, we can confidently look for His provision—He never leaves us on our own.

God's quiet whisper to me:

_____

_____

_____

_____

_____

_____

_____

_____